24

JOHANNES SACA

To order additional copies of this book, contact:
Xlibris
1-888-795-4274
www.Xlibris.com
Orders@Xlibris.com
783755

This book is for Time:

Past,
Present,
Future.

1.

1994

I was born after,
And I was born before.

It just depends on who You are.

2.

PHANTOM

I am my own ghost.

I am my own shadow;
I am the invisible, visible…
I am indivisible.

I am divided.
I am a house;
I am my temple.
I am religion:
I am their words / I am my voice
Repeating their words.

I am the sound;
I know no glory.
I am profound;
I am empty.
I am a hollow masterpiece.

I am supernatural:
Afraid to be common,
Afraid to become.

3.

TRIUMPH, IMAGINED

In daydreams, I hear applause.

It sounds like thunder:
Waves of sound,
Praise unleashed,
A hurricane of worship;
The walls cannot contain their admiration.

I take a bow,
I let the moment sink its teeth
Into my shattered heart.

What is my performance?

There is a light above me.
There is only light above

                              me.

I am afraid of pig's blood.

4.

CONCRETE JUNGLE

Allow this man to dream,
As he dreams of New York.

Young,
vain,
vulnerable,
broken,
arrogant,
illuminated,
UNDISPUTABLY GIFTED,
audacious,

Driven by ART.

How is this man
Excluded from that grand arena?

I follow every sign and
I pluck roses from their stems,
Chocking on cyanide
From a Big Apple.

5.

CAR / COFFIN

I heard the door slam shut
And saw black:
Suffocating in minimalism,
Reaching out for him…
Touching the screen.

I have never felt more human,
Now that I know
How it feels to die.

6.

TEETH

No one fears my teeth:
Too clean to bear evidence,
Not sharp enough to warn.

My bark is musical,
My bite is gentle;
My silence is your weapon.

I am motionless
(statuesque)
A victim of your neglect.

I alone have defined myself:
Capable of violence,
Oppressed by innocence,
Fear of consequence,
And lack of experience.

I am breaking under the weight of expectation.

7.

ICE

The day we define our matter,

With intention and affirmation,
Strong in our identity,

We will matter.

8.

FLAME

To burn a broken heart
Is to set fire to counterfeit.

9.

TOBACCO

Walls composed of human backbones
Trained to stand upright,
Cigarettes smoked years ago
Left ghosts in burning light,
Shells of bullets,
Glass and letters
Hidden in the sand;
I crash into the burning light, I
capture smoke in my hands,
Clasping my hands together
Trying to imprison consequence.

I lose even in these trivial moments,
Smoke seeping through my digits,
Back into the air I breathe,
And I breathe in this consequence
And imprison myself.

I am solid, I am cold,
I am alive,
Immortalized by language.

I have learned to glorify myself
With words.

10.

INTERMISSION: A PRAYER

I am misunderstood
When I speak;
I am misunderstood
When I am silent.

Therefore, I save my words for
Poetry
And pray without religion
To be understood.

11.

PARALLELS

I used to dream of a twin
Who lived an alternate version of my life.

My onyx roots, bleached
Like a tainted night…
Invaded by glamour,
Holding every star accountable
For its death.

Art on my skin,
Ink / messages / illustrations
Proving a wild history
I can only write about.

(The writer, written on)

A beating, eager heart
Pounding passionately
To the beat of a strange melody,
Content in its role:
The life force of an artist
With an iconic, faultless

                              Voice.

And here I am,
Praised for mastering voice
On paper
While my adorned, adored twin
Receives applause.

12.

FEAR OF PUBLICITY

Oh dear…

What have I gotten myself into?

I have exposed my words to You
And now You will write about me.

You will criticize the pages I have birthed
And my agony will be scrutinized by the masses.

I have transformed myself into Fame
By simply exposing my desire for it.

I detest the tabloids.

I ingest the tabloids.

I am just like You.

13.

FEAR OF INFLUENCE

I call myself wise,
The same way a prophet calls himself reliable.

I fear a false prophet,
Yet the prophet does not fear himself.

He who deceives intentionally will perish at the hands of
the deceived, enlightened.

But I shall continue to call myself wise,
For without wisdom, I would perish from the cruelty of
My own hands.

14.

PARALLELS, REVISITED

Am I living his life
Or am I trying to live his life
By killing myself?

15.

FEAR OF FADING

All I ever wanted was to be

visible.

Now, here I am:
The dreamer, awakened
By applause,
Glorified by his enemies,
Adored to

death.

I pity my fears,
So thirsty for attention.

I quench their thirst
By murdering my liver,
Living for lunacy.

Will they still love me when I heal?

16.

FEAR ITSELF

It's there…
In the corner,
Breathing through its pores,
Watching me
Watching it,
Waiting to strike.

If I make any sudden move,
It will grip my ankle
With a thick and determined tentacle,
Taking me with it
Into its spacious darkness
Where stars go to die.

I remain still,
Engaging in a staring contest with my tormentor,
Frozen in asylum.

I may only have conversations with walls here,
But I may not speak of The Fear:
The moment I acknowledge its existence,
It will exist in You too.

17.

ALIVE

I swear,
I must be made of steel.
I can brace myself
Against the hurricane's vicious force
Without bending,
And I will survive
The unpredictable nature of life.

18.

NOT A GIRL, NOT YET A WOMAN

She is the container and the contained.

She turns herself into vodka
And drinks herself twice,
Three times,
Empty and full at once
With eyes
Haunted by memories
Suppressed,
repressed,
expressed all at once by her existence.

She weighs nothing and carries everything.

She navigates her own darkness
By drinking herself too many times to count...
And she crashes, rises, crashes, rises,
Crashes, rises,
Crashes.

She burns and desires to vanish
Afraid of her flames.

She extinguishes herself with holy water
And poisons her veins with identity.

19.

AN AMERICAN CRISIS

All of these obscenities:
Bullets littered on the sidewalks,
Pale solid ground
(foundation)
Burdened by a new and deadly history.

All of these tragic impulses
Of mankind
Surround us
In schools,
Nightclubs,
Shopping centers,
Airplanes,
Vegas,
Bedrooms.

Everywhere is somewhere that could be
Next.

There is a pattern here,
And we should not require

$

To honor our conscience.

I want hope to carry me through,
But now that I have lived and know that I will not live forever,
I must face the truth, even when it is inconvenient.

We are an unfinished chapel
Damned by our architecture.

20.

WHO IS REGRET?

A vote cast in the wrong direction,
A bullet succeeding in its purpose,
A shot of tequila on a date with a stranger,
Six shots of tequila anywhere,
Sleeping with the tequila inside you,
Allowing a stranger inside you,
Living with a stranger inside you,
Waking up nine months later with a stranger in your arms,
Naming a stranger,
Raising a stranger,
Loving a stranger,
Being a stranger to her, who lived in your womb,
Being a stranger to him,
To Him,
To Yourself.

Who is regret…
If he regrets
You,
You regret
Him,
He regrets her,
She regrets him and you,
And you and him
Regret tequila?

21.

ADMIT ONE (TRUTH)

I preach,
But I do not often practice.

I am not the saint you worship.

If I must be honest,
My choices would have been different years ago…
If only I had been brave.

I would have sinned repeatedly,
Just to prove that I could.

I would have made my own mistakes,
Instead of having them made for me.

I would have created life,
Instead of fearing life.

22.

LONDON

I walked through you when I was 19,
I walked through you when I was 22,
I walked through you and I wondered
How I ever lived without you.

It felt as if the only time
I ever lived was in you,
How did you feel about me?
Was I remarkable, was I valued?

Did I love you for your history
Or for who you are today?
Did I love you more than my own country
Will ever love me?

Well, I must really love you…
You're the subject of my poetry,
But so is what I fear,
And so is what I hate.

23.

VERSIONS

This is my heartbeat
These are my words
This is my cry for help
This is my battle cry
This is my rebellion
This is for my brothers
This is for my sisters
This is for their captors
This is me, ending the silence
This is me, heart unbroken
This is me, speaking
To fools,
To scholars,
To corpses,
To the interrupted youth
And their elders in protest.

Listen.

Listen to each other's voices,
Listen to each other's words,
Listen to each other's songs,
Immerse yourself in prose and verse.

Our views are always wrong
If we only hear ourselves.
Listen to your country's heart,
Listen to its fire burn.
Sing its praises to your mother,
Tell her everything you've learned,
Tell her you've been listening,
Tell her everything you've heard.
Listen to each other's mothers,
Listen to women, diverse,
Listen to their stories,
Pay attention, even if it hurts.

Live gratefully, be thankful
For people who don't look like you,
Think like you,
Act like you,
Love like you,
Talk like you,
Sound like you,
Worship like you,
Like you.

Be comfortable enough
In your skin
To respect your neighbor's skin.

This is our truth:

We have never been black,
white,
brown,
immigrants,
gay,
straight,
cis,
trans,
male,
female,
gods,
messiahs…

You are simply human,
Like me,
Like every race and creed and couple you judge,
Like our parents,
Like our children,
Like our enemies,
Like our friends…

VERSIONS.

24.

FACT

I am alive
Because I am worth living for.

CPSIA information can be obtained
at www.ICGtesting.com
Printed in the USA
BVHW08*1158290818
525941BV00006B/17/P